Perfect Worlds

Artistic Forms & Social Imaginaries

Perfect Worlds

Artistic Forms & Social Imaginaries

vol. 1

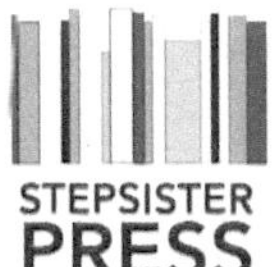

Michael Workman

Published by StepSister Press, 600 S. Crescent Avenue, Park Ridge, IL, U.S.A
stepsisterpress.org

ISBN: 978-1-7326989-1-8

References to internet websites were accurate at the time of writing. Neither the author nor StepSister Press is responsible for URLs that may have expired or changed since the manuscript was prepared.

Library of Congress CIP Data available upon request.

Cover and interior design by Lauren Dacy.
This book was typeset using Adobe Caslon Pro, Filosofia, and Park Lane typefaces and is printed on acid-free paper by Ingram Spark.

For Tristan

CONTENTS

Acknowledgments   11

Introduction   15

Kurt Vonnegut   33

Jenn Freeman (aka Po'Chop)   49

Ayako Kato   58

Shirin Neshat   64

Jamal "Lightbulb" Oliver   69

Michelle Kranicke   75

Jose Santiago Perez   93

Karen Finley   98

Ginger Krebs   113

Precious Jennings   130

Pidgeon Pagonis   147

John Waters 156

Jacinda Ratcliffe 162

Bill Ayers 169

Jeez Loueez 188

Daniel Bozutzky 193

Rosé Hernandez 205

Young Jean Lee 211

Claire Tancons 213

Darling Shear 218

Laurie Anderson 228

J'Sun Howard 235

Allen Moore 247

Bebe Miller 256

Nic Kay 260

Aaron Hughes & Amber Ginsburg 267

Deborah Hay 278

Joshua Ishmon   283

Carole McCurdy   290

Kiam Marcello Junio   297

Kerry James Marshall   303

About the Author   308

Acknowledgments

I'LL BE AS BRIEF AS POSSIBLE HERE, but it's inconceivable I would have been capable of producing this volume, little less a three volume series, without the assistance, support and encouragement of a small, inner circle of people who have lifted me up, encouraged me, gently and lovingly let me know when I was wrong, and upon whose shoulders I stand in eking out this modestly hopeful collection. Foremost among them is my son, Tristan Nathaniel Workman, whose pure joy for life, imagination and decency has carried me through many a difficult year, and who I love with all my heart. His mother Marie Walz, an early partner in life and in the life of the mind, a clever and witty artist who I am proud to still call a friend, off and on. No amount of attempt to lay honorifics upon each named here will soften the crass roll of the credits, insufficient as it is for how dear and powerful the thread of gratefulness is I continuously feel for each whose DNA is involved in the conception of this project. I hope you'll all excuse the flaw in that. Thanks, however, should immediately also go to Annie Heckman and her StepSister Press, whose willingness to champion this project is why you're holding it in your hands right now at all.

I certainly wouldn't have this volume or any of these years of chances to share ideas with anyone without the go-ahead of my longest serving editors, Jan and Brian Hieggelke, many of the writings throughout the series originally having appeared in their now-monthly magazine, *Newcity*, Chicago's art and cultural paper of record. In fact, I've grown so much through their years of kindness, careful cultivation and wise interdictions in ways I thought I'd figured out, and through them realized I hadn't at all.

Kevin Williams at the *Chicago Tribune* was kind enough to raise the volume on my byline while the budget held, Katie Kitamura who edited me thoughtfully at *Contemporary*, and then wrote about my misadventures in redistributing the means of distribution in the *New York Times*. Michele Robecchi and Aaron Moulton at *Flash Art*, Kathryn Hixson at the *New Art Examiner*. Through the *Examiner* crowd I met James Yood, who died this year and who fiercely encouraged me to write criticism, describing me as like "one of those bugs that treads over watery surfaces, making its way by sensing what's going on around it," and, "light on art history," which sent me in a terror adding to the ballast. Jim died the day I'm writing this. Lately, my Movement Matters editors, starting with Tempestt Hazel at *Sixty Inches From Center*, and now Lauren Warnecke at her blog *Art Intercepts*, where she works when not writing in her official role as dance critic at the *Chicago Tribune*. Eric Lorberer, my voice on the other end at *Rain Taxi*, has kept me foraging for new ideas, some of which appear in this volume. Proud associations, all.

It's hard always being at sea on an idea, which is the best way for it to proceed to proof, of course, and along the way, I think of close and influential others who I've subjected to my endless sound-boarding. I'm sure that's why I've not heard from you all in awhile, and I'm sure you know who you are.

My experience of the lectures with Charles Taylor were formative for me, and I'm in a great deal of debt to his ideas and the profound scope of understanding they represent. I would be remiss for not acknowledging his influence on my thought. I also owe a debt to Jacques Derrida, for welcoming the public into his lectures, which I sat in on in the same period of my life, and realized the performativity of philosophic discourse was something I hadn't invented. Through their work and that of Habermas, my focus shifted to the matter of a public identity, and those experiences continue to have transformative effects on me. I note their ideas and positions as they occur in the text, and those of a great many others.

Uncited here are also a great many unofficial relationships without which I would be neglectful to omit recognizing as equally formative to this project over the years. My family is mostly chosen, though that includes my sisters Malissa, Michelle, brother Matthew and the scattered other members, in its continuing diasporic flight from the lesser-desirable effects of clannish roots. There are friends who've provided the sole light in difficult moments, hopscotching through time to support one another as needed, even across great oceans of absence. Mike Newirth and Elizabeth Stigler. Ana Arevalo. Sarah Best. Frank DiCostanzo. Naomi Miller. Karen Leick. J. Niimi. John Beer. Ed Steinhauer (hope Berlin has been good to you)! Mat Rappaport. David Sundry and Michelle Kranicke. Mark Tschaepe, the monster of all friends, always willing to lift me up. Others among my innermost circles. My grandmother Treva, who I miss still. All of you I talk with on Facebook every day.

As a matter of procedural housekeeping, I also wish to acknowledge I have edited each of the works included with the intention of collapsing differences between speakers, geographic and spatial distances, though it's obvious who the questioner and subjects are throughout. This hopefully provides a more socially de-centered view of the dialogue taking place, though I admit it's a conceit directly inspired by the stripping away of the interviewer's questions in Studs Terkel's *Working*. My aesthetic target here was to give the reader a sense of hearing the voice inside their *own* head, as if listening to the language without hearing it spoken aloud. Additionally, tense and person may also at times shift, as do pronouns, in the hopes that there's some sense of this series of volumes as a product of the living language spoken by these thirty-one other artists.

Introduction

These collections of fragments and conversations, essays and ephemera are stitched together from a desire to listen to what other artists were saying and thinking, and to discover what I could about the interests and values that define them in the modern world. Written over a span of more than 20 years, though many are recent, they've appeared with, I believe, very decent-minded publications, and with editors I deeply admire, all of who allowed me to ask questions through my work, and through it to also question my own thoughts as I was having them in the moment. Among them, what is a "self?" for me, has always been tied up with those definitions of who was *permitted* full standing as a human being in society, as that definition has been encoded into laws, into policy, into how we interact with one another socially, and how public opinion may or may not actively play a role in the formation of these standards of conduct. Especially as concerns art, in all its forms. Artists have always been important to how ideas are transmitted to the public and by fiat of this, of course, who was *excluded* from our definitions of those worthy of acceptance.

Deeply flawed, self-awareness as a prerequisite to participation has been the best precept for any sort of visibility within the polis, in some sense, we moderns so far seem capable of devising, though we've always known this was an ongoing matter of refining our past understanding of it. For much of human history, our sense of selfhood was rooted in notions of a public presence endowed by ownership of property. Rooted in ancient Greek and Roman systems, as Habermas wrote, "status in the *polis* was therefore based upon status as the unlimited master of an *oikos*,"[1] and of the inevitable customs, conventions and *nomos* that came along with livestock holdings in slaves, women, and other animals, symbolizing their control over the reproduction of life.

> The bourgeois public sphere emerged historically in conjunction with a society separated from the state. The "social" could be constituted as its own sphere to the degree that on the one hand the private realm as a whole assumed public relevance. The general rules that governed interaction between people now became a public concern.[2]

It's irreconcilable in many ways, these two spheres, except for how *'the rules that governed interaction between people'* then began to assume an unfolding modern primacy against the standards of conduct of the previous moral orders. This sphere, a precursor to the formulation of English estates that came together to form the parliamentary system, continued to echo the rote devaluation of whole spectrums of citizenry as less than equals. It's not until the Model Parliament of 1295, and its addition of the laypeople was incorporated, that we see the clear emergence of the basis for what would later become the House of Commons.

---

1 Habermas, Jurgen, *The Structural Transformation of the Public Sphere; An Inquiry into a Category of Bourgeois Society* (translated by Thomas Burger with the assistance of Frederick Lawrence, MIT Press, 2001, p. 127.
2 Ibid., p. 127.

About the Author

C.A. (Catherine Anne) Klug is primarily a children's author, with the bestselling *The Sought Six: The Sterling Cone* to her name. That said, she does enjoy writing more poetic prose from time to time. During the coronavirus pandemic, many thoughts of varying depth entered her mind, and after a while, she started writing them down.

Catherine hails from Ontario, Canada, where she works as a part time librarian, part time author. She has always known she wanted to be an author, writing her very first book at the age of 5 and never looking back. While writing books truly is her favourite thing to do, she also enjoys horseback riding, golf, completing word searches in record time, and relaxing with a steaming cup of coffee.

Follow Catherine on social media, **@caklugofficial**, or visit **www.caklugofficial.com**